Marquetry

BARRON'S

Original title of the book in Spanish: *Marquetería*
© Parramón Ediciones, S.A., 1999. World Rights
Published by Parramón Ediciones, S.A., Barcelona, Spain

Text: Vicenç Gibert, Josep López, and Jordi Ordoñez
Step-by-step: Joan Ordoñez and Jordi Ordoñez
Series design: Carlos Bonet
Photography: Gabriel Serra

Translated from the Spanish by Michael Brunelle
and Beatriz Cortabarria

All inquiries should be addressed to:
Barron's Educational Series, Inc.
250 Wireless Boulevard
Hauppauge, New York 11788
http://www.barronseduc.com

Library of Congress Catalog Card No.: 00-101640
International Standard Book No. 0-7641-5244-0

Printed in Spain

9 8 7 6 7 5 4 3 2 1

TABLE OF CONTENTS

INTRODUCTION

Marquetry is the art of combining small fragments of different woods, using their natural colors, tinted wood, shell, mother of pearl, bone, and other materials, to create ornamental designs of varying complexity. This should not be confused with the craft of the woodworker, which deals with techniques of carving and joining one piece of wood to another. Marquetry deals with pieces of veneer set into one another on the same plane, creating a smooth and even surface that will later be adhered to a support, which is the body of a piece of furniture or object that is to be decorated.

The techniques of marquetry originated in the Middle Ages, coming from the Moslem world. The Arabs were true masters and precursors of this beautiful craft. In the beginning, marquetry was based on a very geometric style that combined wood with ivory strips and mother-of-pearl details; over time it evolved towards a more figurative style based on nature and the current decorative pictorial styles. The craft became very popular in the Low Countries, and was adapted to the decorative movements of the period, from Louis XIV to Louis XVI, thanks to the great furniture makers of the time that were working in the court. Animal and vegetable motifs were widely popular, combining various natural and tinted woods, which influenced the styles of German, English, Spanish, and Spanish American furniture.

Today, the craft of marquetry is practiced by a few artisans that jealously guard the secrets of the noble profession, and are proud to belong to a select group that remain true to its traditions. Upon entering a marquetry workshop, one has the feeling that time has stood still, observing the meticulous work of the artisan, his slow and precise movements, and the fine, accurate cutting of the saw. The order of the placement of the pieces is used to form a tapestry of colors with different woods, each carefully selected to create the most beautiful decorations.

This book presents the principle secrets of marquetry, from the most popular working techniques to the different kinds of wood veneer. We also show different projects, made by a master craftsman, that demonstrate step-by-step how each piece is developed. Each is devised with the goal of keeping readers from getting lost during the various steps and helping them create either an exact copy or their own version of the final model being demonstrated. We will assume that readers possess the required level of confidence and experience if they are attempting to improvise based on the project.

Compiling this book has been a satisfying experience for the authors, since they are helping to spread the word on a prestigious craft about which little is written. At the same time, the book gives us an idea of the important role played by marquetry in the history of furniture.

Vicenç Gibert i Armengol

THE CRAFT OF MARQUETRY

The word *marquetry* probably comes from the French term *marquer*, which means to squeeze or press. Nowadays, marquetry defines the art of arranging and placing different pieces of wood veneer to create ornamental designs (floral and geometric shapes, pictorial scenes, etc.) that complement the decoration of a piece of furniture or other wood object.

These pieces of veneer can be combined with other materials like mother-of-pearl, ivory, copper, pewter, etc., according to the needs or the taste of the craftsman.

Historically, in inlay work done on furniture, the spaces or hollows were made using chisels and gouges, which are the most widely-used tools in marquetry, and then pieces of other kinds of wood were inlaid. Today, however, the craftsman usually works with veneer or sheets of wood in bright colors that are cut out with small saws and, after assembling the design, he bonds them to a base or wood board.

A large studio is needed for marquetry work, with enough space to amply accommodate several boards set on sawhorses. They should be placed in the order of the work being

1. This marquetry workshop is furnished with a large board supported on sawhorses, and shelves to store materials.

2. Storage area for the veneer. Veneer should be stacked to prevent damage and arranged by type, category, and color.

3. Different kinds of veneer with beautiful coloring.

carried out. Since all of the work is organized on the boards, to begin with, the craftsman considers the design and the veneers to be used, as well as the possibility of adding other materials like mother-of-pearl or some type of metal. Next, the primary and secondary colors and veneers are chosen, and finally, different combina-tions are arranged until arriv-ing at the intended design.

The workshop should have shelves for storing and classi-fying the different kinds of wood veneer.

The pedal-operated bow saw, which is a variation of the scroll saw, is perhaps the tool that best characterizes the craft of marquetry. Although electric saws exist, master craftsmen continue to use the manual version, which, when controlled by the foot, is capable of cutting pieces with great precision and at the appropriate speed according to whether the part being cut is straight, curved, or changing direction. The saw blade used is known as a piercing blade. Often the craftsman will build his own scroll saw, adjusting the parts and mechanisms according to the requirements of his work.

A guillotine cutter is very useful to have in the work-shop for cutting strips or squaring the edges of veneer that must be joined.

It is also very helpful to have a press handy to apply the pressure necessary to bond marquetry designs to their bases, whether the base is a board for a picture, a door, or a table top.

While the objects we have mentioned cover the basic needs of a professional mar-quetry workshop, the quan-tity and size of the equipment used will vary, depending on the level of industrialization of the workshop.

4. The pedal-operated bow saw is the basic tool used for creat-ing large works. The triangular piece at the base is the pedal that moves the saw mechanism.

5. A large industrial cutter for cutting strips and stacks of wood veneer.

6. Large mechanical presses in a single frame. They are used for pressing pieces of great size and for bonding veneer.

7. Pictorial representation of a seascape. The entire seascape was made with asymmetrical pieces of different colored veneers.

8. Decorative marquetry using floral motifs. In this case, the veneers used were colored with dyes.

9. Symmetrical design created by contrasting three different colored veneers.

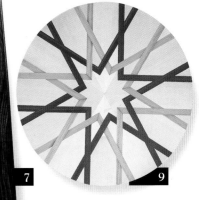

OVERVIEW OF MATERIALS

Today, the most commonly used material in marquetry is wood veneer. There are other secondary materials used to complement the veneer, giving it a more luxurious character. Examples include brass, silver, gold, zinc, tortoise shell, mother-of-pearl, ivory, and horn.

Veneer

Veneer is a thin sheet of wood with a thickness that usually varies from 1/64 to 1/32 inch (0.4 to 0.8 mm). Veneer of greater thickness is also made, and is often used in the manufacture of furniture.

There are two main groups of veneer: veneer used as a decorative covering and structural veneer. The latter is used to make layered boards or plywood.

Veneer is cut from trees, but its fibers differ depending on the part of the tree it comes from. When the veneer comes from the trunk, the fibers are long, straight, and even. If it is taken from the base of the tree, the fibers can take various forms. There are species, like mahogany, that sprout two trunks when they first sprout, which can create a very beautiful and unique pattern in veneer. Finally, some veneers are cut from the roots of the tree; in this case, the fibers are usually arranged in such a way that they create some patterns that are very appreciated in marquetry. Keep in mind that, since veneer is a covering, and therefore is decorative, low-quality woods are never used in its manufacture.

Veneer can have different names according to the arrangement of its grain:

Veneer with straight or regular grain. These have fibers that are nearly straight lines, without much waviness or color variation.

Curly veneer. These are the veneers with fibers that are wavy and that show a variation in the color.

Mottled veneer. In this type of veneer, the grain usually has an irregular, wavy figure.

Bird's eye veneer. This results when the grain forms small knots that are very close together.

Crotch veneer. This veneer comes from the crotch or fork where the branches grow from the trunk. It presents a variety of delightful figures with a pronounced coloration.

Different processes are employed in the production of veneer. Sawn veneer is cut with a large circular saw, creating pieces with a thickness of 3/64 to 13/64 inch (1 to 5 mm). Sliced veneer is cut with a large blade resembling that of a plane to create sheets that run from 1/32 to 1/16 inch thick (0.8 to 1.5 mm). Finally, rotary cut veneer is made by a machine with a blade that cuts a continuous sheet as the trunk is rotated on a lathe. This system creates veneer that is 1/250 to 1/125 inch thick (0.1 to 0.2 mm).

1. Veneer cut from the wood of the sapele tree.

2. Oak burl veneer.

3. Elm burl veneer.

4. Amboina burl veneer.

Backing boards

Boards are used as the backing for all designs created in marquetry; they preserve, protect, and strengthen them. A piece of marquetry not attached to a backing can suffer irreparable damage.

The thickness of the backing boards can vary greatly; the most common is 1/4 inch (5 mm).

The backing boards can be manufactured in several ways:

Chipboard. Also known as particle board, it is made with wood chips coated with a synthetic resin adhesive and pressed to the required thickness.

Fiberboard. The type that is most commonly used is called medium density fiberboard (MDF). It is made from dry wood fibers soaked in synthetic resin and then pressed.

Plywood. Plywood is manufactured using sheets or thin layers of wood that are glued and pressed together.

5. Veneer cut from baboen burl.

6. Veneer cut from poplar burl.

7. Veneer cut from amboina burl.

8. From left to right: sheets of copper, zinc, and brass.

9. Clockwise from upper left: pieces of ivory, animal bones, and mother-of-pearl.

10. From left to right: chipboard, fiberboard, and plywood.

COMMONLY USED TOOLS AND EQUIPMENT

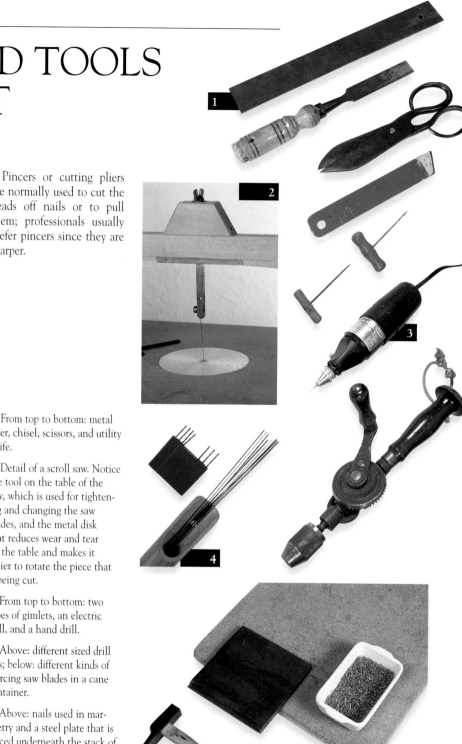

The tools and equipment used in marquetry are many and are as varied as the processes employed. Nevertheless, they can be generally classified as tools and machines for cutting, boring, striking and pulling, holding, scraping and cutting, and pressing.

Cutting tools

All tools used to cut or saw any material used in marquetry belong to this category. Besides chisels, scissors, and utility knives, the following should be pointed out:

Pedal-operated bow saw. This consists of a frame to which is attached a small, long saw blade with very fine teeth, which should always be angled downwards. The blades can be of two types: flat and with teeth or cylindrical. Professionals usually prefer the former for its ease of use when it comes to making straight cuts. The blades are classified according to the width of the blade; they range from 3/64 to 1/8 inch (1 to 3 mm). Their lengths vary also, ranging from 8 to 10 inches (20 to 25 cm).

Fret saw. These are used for cutting out small designs. They consist of a metal arc with a handle at one end, to which is attached a saw blade like the ones previously described. They should always be under tension to cut correctly.

Guillotine cutter. This consists of a large sharp blade attached to a frame at one end. At the other end, there is a handle so it can be moved like a lever. It is usually used for squaring the ends of large sheets of veneer.

Boring tools

Generally speaking, the quickest and simplest way of making a hole in a piece of veneer is to use a nail or an awl. However, when the material is something other than wood, like mother-of-pearl, copper, or brass, a hand drill must be used. The drill, which holds a bit, is controlled manually by turning a wheel. Small, low-powered electric drills can also be used, since the materials that are to be drilled are usually thin and soft.

Striking and pulling tools

Striking and pulling tools are grouped together because they are closely related. The most common is the tack hammer, which is used to drive small nails into the stacks of veneer that are to be sawn to ensure they are held together tightly.

Pincers or cutting pliers are normally used to cut the heads off nails or to pull them; professionals usually prefer pincers since they are sharper.

1. From top to bottom: metal ruler, chisel, scissors, and utility knife.

2. Detail of a scroll saw. Notice the tool on the table of the saw, which is used for tightening and changing the saw blades, and the metal disk that reduces wear and tear on the table and makes it easier to rotate the piece that is being cut.

3. From top to bottom: two types of gimlets, an electric drill, and a hand drill.

4. Above: different sized drill bits; below: different kinds of piercing saw blades in a cane container.

5. Above: nails used in marquetry and a steel plate that is placed underneath the stack of veneer when nailing it together. Below: cutting pliers and a hammer.

the main tools used for scraping, cutting, and smoothing the veneer. The first has a wood or plastic handle with a steel blade inserted at one end, which is not sharpened but perfectly straight and without teeth. The second is a tool that is simple and easy to use, which consists of a blade of semi-hardened tempered steel measuring approximately 6 inches by 3 inches and 3/64 inch thick (14 cm by 7 cm, and 1 mm). The burr along its long edges does the cutting.

Pressing tools and machines
Different types of presses are used in marquetry, according to the task and the needs of the craftsman.

Veneering press. This is normally used for gluing veneer. It consists of a solid steel frame with two wood platforms or plates laying on steel rails. The lower platform is stationary, the upper one can be moved.

Book binding press. Used for pressing veneer sheets. The approximate dimensions of the base are 20 inches by 20 inches (50 cm by 50 cm).

Fixed press. This press was specifically designed for pressing veneer. The dimensions of the bed are usually 96 inches by 44 inches (240 cm by 110 cm).

Clamp. This simple tool can perfectly fulfill the duties of a press. This is done by inserting the veneer between two boards and placing enough clamps (at least four, one on each side), to create sufficient pressure.

6. Top to bottom: scraper, tweezers, and awl.

7. Above: veneer hammer; below: wooden veneer hammer. Both are used for applying pressure to veneer to ensure it is completely bonded to the base board.

8. From left to right: steel awl, crosslock tweezers, tweezers, and wood handled awl.

9. Manual press for small pieces of marquetry.

10. Manually controlled stationary press for large marquetry work or veneering.

Holding tools
Tweezers about 4 inches long (10 cm) and an awl are normally used to carefully and accurately hold the small pieces that make up part of a design. These tools are also used to avoid the risk of burns.

Scraping and cutting tools
The scraper and the knife are

PREPARING THE DESIGN

One of the most difficult and complicated tasks is choosing the design to use. Keep in mind that, in the great majority of cases, the objective of the marquetry work is to decorate or complement a piece of furniture of a specific style, and therefore, it should not only go well with it, but it should also add to its beauty and artistic value.

Once the craftsman has achieved a harmonious balance of the various aspects such as style, color, size, and decorative motifs, he can lay out the design after first selecting the most appropriate technique and process for making the design drawing.

It is important to remember that the design should always be made full size. The drawing can be an original creation or a copy. If it is original, it should be started as a sketch made freehand, and later be laid out at full size. If you are working with a copy, it should be enlarged or reduced until arriving at the desired size.

Once the drawing is complete, it is colored with pencils to approximate the tones of the veneers to be used.

Next, the direction of the wood grain is established; if this step is first worked out on paper, time will be saved during the process of making the stack of veneer, which is made prior to cutting out the pieces.

Copying designs

Usually the design to be copied exists as a book illustration because there are so many specialized publications containing design motifs, landscapes, still lifes, etc.

To copy a drawing from a book, the contour and inside lines are traced with an ink pen onto a sheet of paper placed over the illustration. It is a good idea to practice with the pen on a sheet of scratch paper before starting the tracing. This will prevent a shaky hand from affecting the quality of the reproduction.

Next, a photocopy is made on white paper and the original drawn on tracing paper is carefully put into a folder so that it can be used on other occasions. The pieces (or sections) are marked and numbered on the copy of the drawing to record all the different pieces that will become part of the composition. Then, the picture is colored with different colored pencils to imitate the tones of the wood veneers. Finally, the kind and color of the veneers are selected after comparing them with the design drawn on the paper.

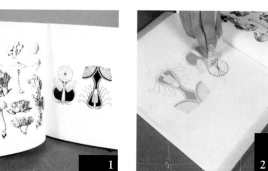

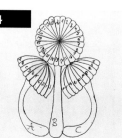

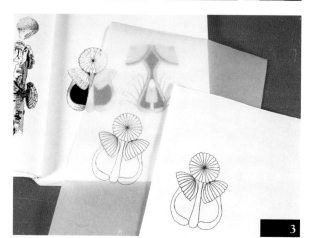

1. A book of reproducible decorative motifs. The pages in the photograph show plant motifs at different scales.

2. The tracing paper is placed over the page of the book and the design is traced with a pencil or an ink pen with a fine point.

3. Compare the original drawing, the copy made on tracing paper, and the photocopy of the tracing on plain white paper.

4. All of the pieces in the chosen design are marked and numbered on the photocopy.

5. Finally, the design and its background are colored.

6. The type and color of veneer is then chosen based on the colored drawing.

Original freehand designs

Creating an original design requires a sense of esthetics and proportion. It is a good idea to make several sketches and, after choosing a design, begin making a drawing of it at full size to aid in the development of the composition of the marquetry.

Geometric designs

If the original drawings are geometric designs, such drawing instruments as a compass, ruler, and square will be required for making the straight and curved lines. If these tools are not used, the freehand drawing will most likely be imprecise and will affect the overall quality of the design.

Again, it is a good idea to practice drawing the geometric shapes beforehand, because, despite their simple appearance, they must follow strict rules of symmetry.

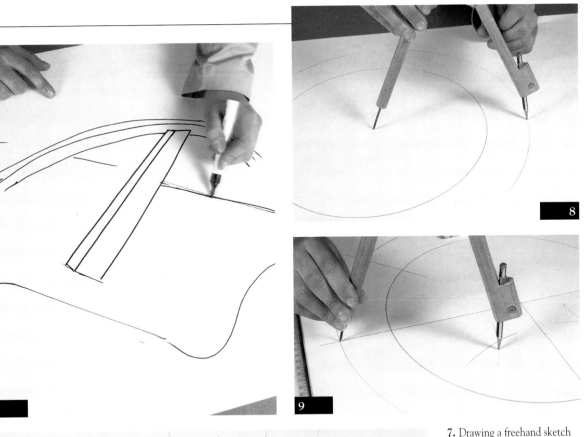

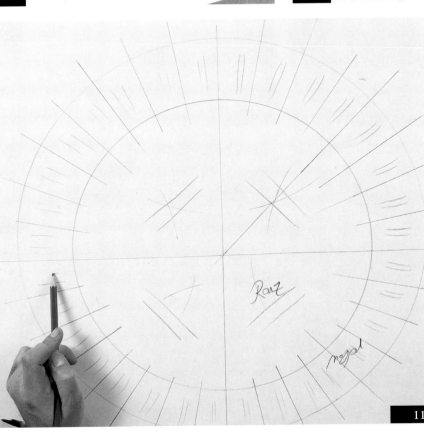

7. Drawing a freehand sketch based on an original idea for a frame.

8. Drawing two concentric circles at full size for a table top, using a carpenter's compass.

9. After drawing the circles, they can be segmented to establish the areas that will be individual pieces of veneer. This is done by dividing the circles into four equal parts, which are then each divided into two.

10. Tracing the bisector with a ruler to divide one of the quadrants of the circle into two equal parts.

11. Coloring and marking the direction of the grain to indicate the individual pieces of veneer.

PREPARING THE VENEER

In the logical process of creating a marquetry composition, the preparation of the pieces of veneer to be cut and assembled immediately follows the choice and creation of the design itself.

To prepare a stack of veneer, each of the pieces must first be backed with sheets of paper that have been brushed with glue. This strengthens the pieces and will keep them from splintering and breaking during the cutting process. Newsprint may be used for this purpose.

The most commonly used product for gluing veneer in marquetry is rabbit skin glue. This type of glue does not penetrate the pores of the wood, but forms a thick film that bonds the two surfaces to be joined. It is sold in the form of flakes, and has an ideal consistency for use with veneer. When put into a container, mixed with water, and then heated in a double boiler, the flakes form a thick glue that is applied using a wide brush or a small artist's paint brush spread evenly over the entire surface.

Next, the drawing of the design is cut out and bonded to a sheet called the master, whose function is to stiffen the design drawing and add thickness to the stack of veneer. This makes it easier for the craftsman to work with the material.

Before making the stack for cutting, all of the pieces are placed in the press for about fifteen minutes, to guarantee a good bond between the papers and veneer. A manual press can be used for this task if permitted by the size of the pieces. In any case, the press must be large enough to press the entire surface of the marquetry at the same time.

Then, the pieces are removed from the press, put in order by color, and nailed together using small marquetry nails. This is done on a wooden board to protect the top of the work table. The nails are inserted about 2 inches (10 cm) apart; their function is to simply keep the sheets from shifting during the cutting process.

Once sheets are nailed together, the nails are hammered, much like a rivet, after first cutting the points off the nails that are coming through the stack. Then the nails are tapped with a hammer where they have been cut off. A steel plate placed underneath the stack will help achieve a solid blow and the rivet effect will be more effective.

In this way the stack of veneer and the drawing of the design are prepared and ready for the cutting of the pieces.

1. The rabbit skin glue is prepared by mixing the flakes with water in a container. Then the mixture is heated in a double boiler until it reaches a viscous consistency.

2. Applying the rabbit skin glue to the entire surface of a sheet of wood veneer with a brush.

3. Next, a piece of paper of larger size is bonded to the side of the veneer that is brushed with glue.

4. Rabbit skin glue is applied to the master sheet. Notice that the veneer is lighter in tone than the previous one.

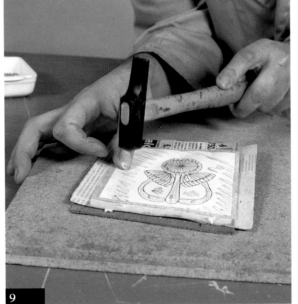

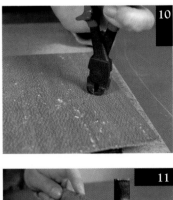

5. After the master sheet is brushed with glue, the drawing of the design is lined up and put into place.

6. Then the prepared sheets of veneer are immediately placed between two boards and the entire stack is placed in a manual press.

7. After about fifteen minutes, the veneer is taken out of the press. Notice that they are different colors.

8. The stack is then prepared using a hammer and nails.

9. It is a good idea to perform this step on a wooden board. Enough nails should be driven in to hold the stack together.

10. Then, the points of the nails that are sticking out are cut off with pincers.

11. Finally, the nails are riveted by striking them with a hammer. The steel plate placed underneath the stack will keep the veneer from being damaged.

CUTTING THE VENEER

After the stacks of veneer are prepared, the pieces laid out in the drawing of the design are cut out.

Generally speaking, a fret saw is used for cutting. Electric scroll saws can also be used; however, since a minimum of force is required to cut veneer, a manual saw is more than sufficient. During the process of cutting out the pieces, the stack itself is moved with the hands, guiding the lines past the moving saw blade. In cases where the design requires cutting out an interior shape, for example, the eyes of a face, it is first necessary to make a hole with a very fine drill bit to pass the saw blade through. A hand drill can be used to make holes in the veneer.

Marquetry or fret saws will work just as well as a pedal-operated bow saw, although the thickness of the veneer should be no greater than 2 inches (5 cm). For correct use of the saws, a support should be placed on the workbench with a v-shaped groove for the saw blade to pass through. It should be held in place with clamps. The tension of the saw blade is adjusted using the thumb screw on the saw. The teeth of the blade should point downward toward the handle, which is at the lower end when the saw is in use.

The veneer can also be cut with blades or a utility knife. Metal straight edges are necessary for precise and long straight cuts, and they can be held to the workbench with clamps. Wood or plastic straight edges are also used, but they wear out quite quickly.

Utility knives are also used when making freehand cuts, mainly on curved pieces of veneer. It is important to keep in mind that cuts made across the grain of the wood can easily cause it to splinter, so great skill is required.

Another tool that is commonly used for cutting veneer is the guillotine cutter. This tool makes very clean linear cuts.

We cannot close this chapter without a warning about the risk associated with using any one of these cutting tools; it is a good idea to be careful, take all the appropriate cautions, and use the tools correctly.

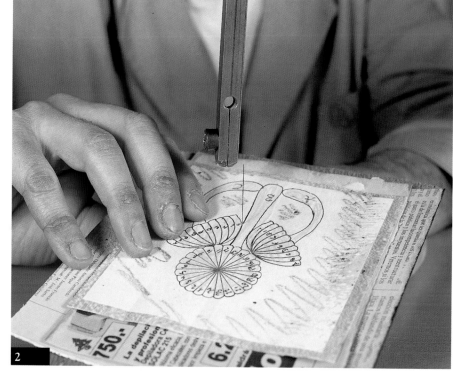

1. To make a hole in the veneer it is best to use a simple hand drill with a small bit. Something should always be placed underneath to protect the top of the work table.

2. The piercing saw blade is passed through the hole made with the hand drill. The teeth of the saw should angle downward.

3. Then, the pedal of the bow saw is put into motion and the process of cutting the different pieces begins.

4. After a piece is cut out, the stack is removed from the saw and the operation is repeated as many times as necessary to cut all of the pieces.

5. Cutting can also be done using a marquetry saw or fret saw. It is necessary to insert the blade and tension it using the wing nuts.

6. Shown here is the correct position of the hands, saw, and pieces for efficient cutting. Also notice the board used as a support. It has a v-shaped groove that allows the saw to pass through.

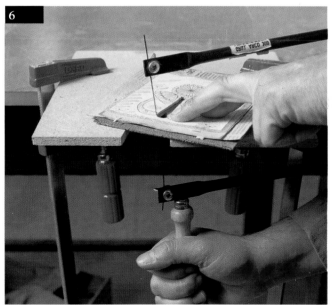

7. Holding a metal straight edge to a board using a clamp to guide a straight cut in the veneer.

8. The utility knife should be guided by a straight edge in order to make a proper cut.

9. Making a square cut in the veneer using a wide chisel.

10. Freehand cutting of a curved shape with a utility knife.

11. The guillotine cutter can be used to make square cuts in the veneer, cutting it into strips of any width.

SHADING TECHNIQUES

Many pieces used in marquetry are shaded, a technique that increases their decorative effect and gives a sensation of volume and depth. Nevertheless, we must keep in mind that the main purpose of marquetry is to create a colorful decorative effect through the use of the natural tones of the veneer on a flat surface, and therefore we recommend not to overdo the shading.

The shading should be done once the veneer is cut. There are several methods used for creating shading:

Hot sand

The most common shading technique consists of introducing the pieces to be shaded in a tray of very fine silica sand previously heated to a high temperature for about five or ten minutes in a shallow metal tray that withstands high temperatures. A piece of veneer should be kept at hand to insert into the sand from time to time to determine the exact moment the sand reaches the ideal working temperature.

Once the sand is hot, the pieces to be shaded are picked up with tweezers and placed in it. It is very important to use tweezers for handling the pieces. After obtaining the desired amount of shading, by varying the exposure time in the sand according to the type of veneer, the pieces are removed from the sand.

The heated wood veneer appears lightly scorched, and the greater or lesser degree of darkness depends on the exposure time. If the piece is left in the sand for too long, there is a risk of burning it and ruining the desired effect.

To create a curved shadow, the surface of the sand is shaped so that only the area to be shaded is covered by it.

It is advisable to carry out the shading process in an organized manner. To do this, all of the pieces to be shaded should be put in a tray where they can be moved from one place to another without the risk of becoming lost.

On occasion, the creation of shading using hot sand can warp the veneer pieces because the natural humidity of the wood is eliminated. Therefore, it is necessary to lightly wet the pieces to make them soft again, and then to put them into the press for five minutes. One very simple and sure way to flatten them out again is to place the wood veneer between two pieces of wood and apply pressure with a clamp.

1. The use of an adjustable electric hotplate is recommended for heating the silica sand to use in the process of shading the pieces.

2. Once the hotplate is plugged in, a metal tray about 1 inch deep (2 or 3 cm) is filled with silica sand and placed on the burner.

3. Notice how shapes can be formed in the very fine silica sand to create curved shading on the veneer.

4. The use of two hotplates can simplify the process in cases where there are many pieces to shade.

5. Notice how tweezers are used to introduce the pieces into the tray of sand. The tweezers are also used to create swirls in the sand that allow the creation of curved shading.

6. The pieces are darkened after just a few seconds. Take a close look at the shading created at the edge that was in contact with the sand.

7. It is very important to stay organized during the process. To do this, the pieces are carefully grouped in a tray.

8. In cases where the pieces have warped due to the effect of the heat, they can be moistened with water using a paint brush.

9. Once the veneer is moistened, it should be placed in a manual press or between two flat boards clamped together.

10. Having been shaded, moistened, and pressed, the veneer pieces are now ready for assembly.

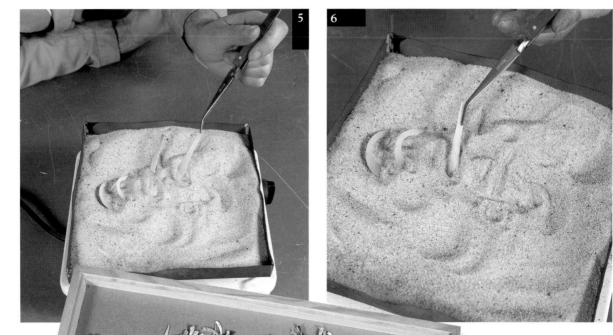

Staining with acids

One very ancient procedure consists of blackening the veneer by applying acids with a fine paint brush. These acids penetrate the interior of the pores of the wood, creating a gradation of varying tones according to the manner in which the acids are applied.

Wood burning

Shading can also be achieved by burning the wood, a technique using an electric soldering iron with a resister that causes the point to become hot. This tool is then used to do the shading. Tips for the wood burning tools are usually available in different shapes: flat, round, pointed, etc.

ASSEMBLING AND MOUNTING PIECES

Assembly

The assembly of the pieces that make up the marquetry work requires a great deal of skill and patience. This is, perhaps, the most delicate operation of the entire process, given the fragility and small size of the pieces. Nevertheless, keep in mind that when the pieces are glued to the backing board, any small breaks become nearly invisible.

The first procedure

First, the stack made up of the veneer must be taken apart. To do so, the heads of the nails that hold the veneer together must be taken off. Then, with great care and the help of a screwdriver, the pieces are separated and placed in an orderly manner on a tray. In landscape compositions, there are usually many varied pieces, and it is of crucial importance to keep them in the correct order.

Once the veneer is taken apart and put in proper order, the piece that will eventually become the frame is fixed to a board, with the side with the paper bonded to it facing up. Since this is just temporary, masking tape or nails can be used to hold it. Meanwhile, a copy of the design on paper is used as a guide during the assembly. The different pieces are mounted into the frame with the papered side up. They should fit into place as if they were pieces of a puzzle. For this, the use of tweezers or an awl is recommended.

When the assembly of all the pieces of the composition is complete, they are glued. First, a piece of paper about the size of the marquetry composition is brushed with rabbit skin glue. Then it is placed over the assembled pieces.

If nails have been used to hold the frame, they should be pushed through the paper and removed with pincers to free the frame from the board. If masking tape has been used, just peel it off. The entire assembly is turned over and the placement of the pieces is checked using an awl. This step is of the utmost importance since a good finish depends on the correct placement of the marquetry pieces.

Next, the assembly is placed between two sheets of paper and two boards and then into a press where it is left to dry. Two weights can also be placed on top of the two boards.

The second procedure

Another procedure for mounting the veneer that is slightly different than that explained above is when a marquetry project is constructed with geometric motifs in which borders and strips are used.

Strips are narrow pieces of wood that measure from 3/64 inch wide (1 mm) or wider and are inserted into the veneering to highlight the work. Borders are usually wider than strips; they can be around 1 1/2 to 2 inches wide (3 to 5 cm).

The strips can be used to create very complex designs and to frame the different compartments of the object being decorated. At the same time they can take the shape of interwoven lines, Greek keys, etc.

Nowadays, very complex and decorative strips are made and can be bought in long pieces in specialized stores.

The function of the borders is the same as the strips; to go around the outside of the decorative design.

Mounting strips is very delicate work since it requires precision. In the first place, masking tape must be placed on a support with the adhesive side facing up; next, the strips, the borders and all of the pieces that make up the geometric design are put into place. Then, a veneering hammer or a regular hammer is pressed with some force against the joints of the veneer.

Mounting

Once assembly is complete, it must be mounted; the assembly of veneers is bonded to a wood backing board. Generally, the marquetry and support are impregnated with white glue, joined together, and placed into a press for several hours.

When the marquetry object is a picture, a simple piece of plywood, fiberboard, or chipboard may be used for backing.

If the marquetry will be placed on furniture, use strong and dependable contact cement for a good bond.

1. Taking apart the stack of veneer by using pincers to remove the nails that hold it together.

2. Separating the veneer with a screwdriver.

3. It is recommended that all of the veneer that make up the stack be separated with great care to prevent surface damage.

4. Design and frames of veneer that will be used for assembly of the different pieces of the composition.

5. The veneer that will serve as the frame is attached to a board using masking tape with the side covered with paper facing up.

6. The frame can also be attached to the board using nails and a hammer.

7. Once the veneer that is used for the frame is attached, the tray of pieces is ready for assembly.

8. Notice that the pieces are carefully arranged and grouped on the tray.

9. With the help of an awl, the pieces are placed in their corresponding places in the frame.

10. View of the pieces perfectly inserted into the frame.

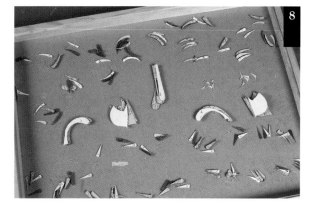

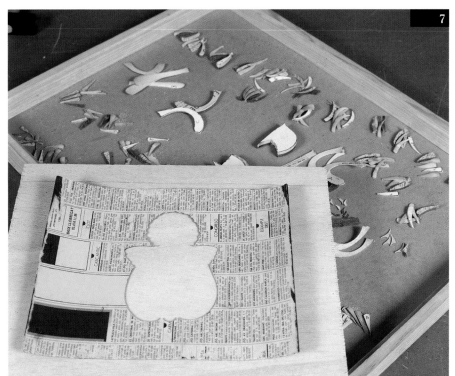

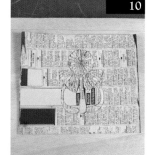

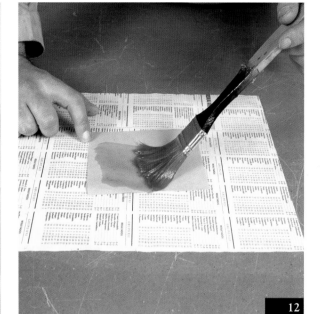

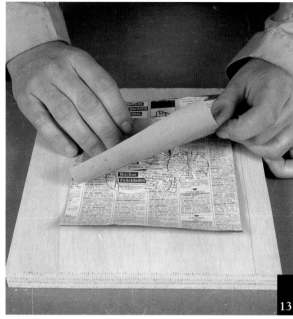

11. Next, a piece of paper approximately the same size as the marquetry should be cut out.

12. The paper is then thoroughly brushed with rabbit skin glue. A paper or a tray should be placed underneath to protect the top of the workbench.

13. Once the paper is covered with glue, it is placed over the assembled marquetry. Make sure it is completely covered.

14. Notice that the nails that hold the frame have pushed through the paper.

15. When the glue has dried, the nails are removed using pincers.

16. When the nails are removed, the marquetry comes free from the board used as a support.

17. The veneer is turned over and the assembly is adjusted using an awl.

18. Then, the assembly is prepared for pressing by placing it between two pieces of paper and two flat boards.

19. A manual press can be used to flatten the pieces, leaving them in place for several minutes.

20. Veneer can also be assembled using masking tape. To do so, the tape should be placed on a board with the adhesive side facing upwards.

21. The sheets of veneer are placed on the strip of masking tape, making sure the edges meet correctly at the joint.

22. Next, a hammer is used to press the pieces of veneer, being careful not to damage them.

23. Then, the veneer is attached to a backing board using white glue.

24. Here, the marquetry work is finally attached to the backing board.

PREPARING THE MARQUETRY FOR FINISHING

After gluing and pressing the marquetry, all that is left to do is to unmask its beauty.

Removing the masking tape and the paper

The veneer should be left for approximately ten hours in the press to dry completely. Then, it can be taken out and all of the masking tape removed by grasping it at one end and pulling it off. This operation can be carried out easily by hand, or at most with a utility knife to lift up the end of the masking tape.

Next, the paper is dampened to make its removal easier. This can be done by taking a sponge soaked in water and lightly wetting all of the paper covering the surface of the marquetry. It is a good idea to use clean water, otherwise it could cause unexpected and unwanted staining on the marquetry. If you wait two or three minutes you will notice the paper becoming wrinkled and the marquetry underneath will begin to show through.

A paint scraper can be used to eliminate what is left of the paper, making very careful back and forth movements on the surface of the marquetry.

Once all of the paper is removed, you will notice that the veneer is damp. It is advisable to wait until it dries before you proceed with the scraping operation. The waiting time will depend on the amount of humidity in the atmosphere and in the piece. If desired, you can accelerate the drying process by sprinkling sawdust over the entire surface; this will absorb some of the humidity still contained in the veneer. Later, the sawdust can be removed with the paint scraper. The use of heat for drying is not a good idea, because the veneer could become scorched or the adhesive could become weakened.

1. Marquetry taken from the press and tools for removing the paper attached to it.

2. To begin, the strips of masking tape are pulled off.

3. The paper is dampened with a water soaked sponge.

4. With the paper wetted, the design of the marquetry shows through.

5. The wetted paper is removed with a spatula, taking care not to damage the wood veneer.

6. This is the marquetry formally covered by the paper.

7. Sawdust is spread over the entire surface in order to accelerate drying of the veneer.

8. The sawdust is removed with the paint scraper.

Scraping

Once the wood is dry, the entire surface is thoroughly scraped. This is done using a scraper blade, strictly following the grain of the wood, since if it were done across the grain the veneer could become loose and damaged.

The basic function of the scraping is to completely eliminate the glue still adhered to the wood and to level the heights of the different veneers used. During the scraping process, some professionals resort to using other tools like chisels to scrape corners and other difficult to reach areas.

Cutting and finishing the outside edge

After the scraping procedure, the perimeter of the marquetry board is cut and edged. The board is normally a little bit larger than needed so that cutting and squaring the veneer and the backing board can be done at the same time. This task is usually done on the pedal-operated bow saw, but using blades that are somewhat wider than those normally used when cutting the veneer. Then, the edges are sanded, and finally a strip of wood veneer is attached with contact cement to create a finished look. Heavier strips of solid wood may also be attached.

9. Scraping a marquetry piece; a picture frame illustrates this step instead of the veneered board. Notice how the scraper is held.

10. Sawing the perimeter of the board with the pedal-operated bow saw.

11. The edges of the board are smoothed using sandpaper and a sanding block.

FINISHING

As is the case in other crafts related to carpentry, the finishing or treatment of the surface of the marquetry is the last step carried out. It is done for the purpose of protecting and beautifying the work. To do this, it is necessary to have a knowledge of the materials and products available on the market, as well as the techniques for their correct use and application.

The finishing process is divided into three phases:

Sanding

This consists of rubbing the surface of wood veneer with sandpaper. There are numerous types of sandpaper available on the market that are basically differentiated by the size of their grit.

Sanding may be done using just the hands, or with the help of a sanding block, or mechanically with power tools specifically designed for this purpose.

Varnishing

This step protects the wood and brings out its beauty. There are many products available on the market for varnishing veneer. Shellac makes a very good finish but is little used nowadays, having been replaced by varnishes that contain a filler as one of their components.

Shellac. This is a varnish available in flakes that is

1. Clockwise from upper left: sanding block, orbital power sander, and scraping blades.

2. Different samples of sandpaper. The lighter the color, the finer the grit.

3. On the left, a varnish with filler; on the right, shellac.

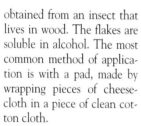

obtained from an insect that lives in wood. The flakes are soluble in alcohol. The most common method of application is with a pad, made by wrapping pieces of cheesecloth in a piece of clean cotton cloth.

Varnish. Today, this is used much more often than shellac, since varnish can be easily applied with wide or fine brushes. Varnish leaves a thin protective coating on the wood.

When the varnish is dry, the surface is again sanded with a fine grained sandpaper. Then, the surface is buffed with fine steel wool to polish the varnish.

Waxing

After buffing the finish, the surface is coated with waxes that have been especially developed for this purpose.

The application of the wax is done with cheesecloth or a cotton cloth, spreading it evenly over the entire surface.

Then the surface is vigorously buffed using a clean and dry cotton cloth.

4. Manually sanding the marquetry on a wooden picture frame. The dust created by the sanding is very fine.

5. Varnishing the frame with the aid of a brush.

6. Hand sanding with very fine grit sandpaper after the varnishing procedure.

7. The surface is vigorously rubbed with steel wool in the same direction as the wood grain.

8. The application of wax using cheesecloth.

9. In order to get a glossy finish, the piece must be buffed with a clean and dry cotton cloth.

RECTANGULAR LID

*T*his exercise demonstrates how to create a symmetrical marquetry piece with the representation of a compass star. During this process, we use a utility knife instead of a saw to make perfectly defined linear cuts. At the same time, the mounting procedure is noticeably different from the one normally used; the veneer is not prepared in a stack, but is placed directly on the drawing for cutting.

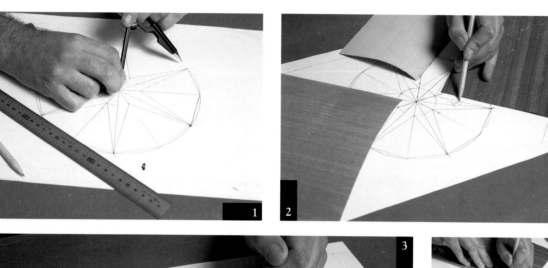

1. To begin, a full-size drawing is made of the design to be created in marquetry.

2. Next, the desired combination of veneers is chosen for the marquetry piece, noting on the drawing the type of wood to be used. In this exercise, we are using coral, sycamore, etimoe, beech, and oak wood veneers.

3. The drawing is colored with tones close to those of the veneers, indicating the direction of the grain at the same time.

4. Then, the coral veneer pieces are marked following the direction of the grain as indicated in the drawing. To do so, the veneer should be placed over the drawing and the line for cutting marked with a ruler and pencil with a sharp point.

5. The veneer is cut with a blade and a metal straight edge. Notice that this is done on a wood board so as not to damage the table top.

6. Once all the coral and sycamore pieces that make up the star are cut, they are attached to a piece of paper with white glue to make it easier to mark the rest of the pieces. This can be done directly on the drawing of the design, being careful not to apply an excessive amount of glue.

7. Press the pieces firmly with your fingers in order to make them bond well. It is very important to align them perfectly.

8. Next, in the same manner as previously described, the background of the star is marked. It will be made with oak veneer.

9. The pieces are attached and adjusted on the paper. The pattern created by the lines of the grain is called diamond matching.

10. The quartered background of the marquetry lid is marked on another piece of paper, again indicating the direction of the grain of each piece. In this case, we are using etimoe wood.

11. Then the wood is marked and cut with the help of a metal straight edge and a utility knife.

12. When the quarter sections have been cut and aligned, they are joined in pairs with tape.

13. Even pressure is applied with the veneer hammer so that the tape is completely bonded to the pieces of veneer.

14. A metal straight edge is placed on the veneer and one edge is cut straight and square with a utility knife.

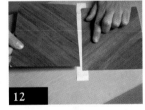

15. The previously described operation is repeated with the remaining pair, and then the two pieces are joined.

16. The extra paper is removed from the star using a cutting blade.

17. Then the star is placed on the sheet of quartered veneer and attached with small nails using a hammer.

18. Next, the perimeter of the star is traced on the quartered background with a sharp pencil.

19. A reference point is marked on two pieces of veneer to help place the star in the same position later.

20. The star is removed and the background veneer is cut on the marked line using a metal straight edge and a blade.

21. Then, it is turned over and masking tape is applied to hold the star in place temporarily.

22. The star is placed on the background veneer. Notice how the reference marks that were made earlier are now aligned.

23. Using a square, a metal straight edge and a utility knife, the rest of the edges of the quartered background are squared.

24. Then, strips of beech veneer approximately 1 1/4 inches wide (3 cm) are cut to create a frame.

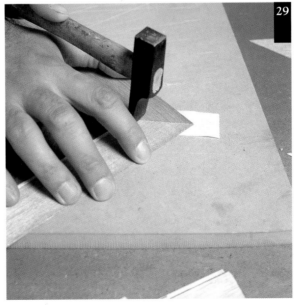

25. Masking tape is placed around the perimeter on the back of the quarters. On top, a strip is attached.

26. Next, the frame pieces are put in place overlapping the corners, making sure the pieces are perfectly aligned.

27. The joints are aligned by pressing firmly on the pieces of veneer with a hammer.

28. The corners are cut at a 45 degree angle with a metal straight edge and a utility knife.

29. After removing the extra pieces of veneer, the joint at the corner is pressed with the hammer.

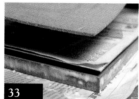

30. Once the veneer is finished, proceed to glue it to the backing board. This can be done by applying white glue on both surfaces with a wide brush.

31. The two surfaces are joined.

32. They are held in place with a few nails to keep them from moving.

33. A sheet of paper is placed on top and covered with a layer of cork. The entire assembly is put into a press to ensure a perfect bond.

34. After several hours, the board is taken from the press and the temporary nails are removed.

35. Next, the paper that covers the marquetry is dampened with a sponge soaked with water so it can be removed.

36. After five minutes, begin removing the paper at one side of the marquetry using a scraper.

37. The process is continued on the center of the marquetry in the same manner.

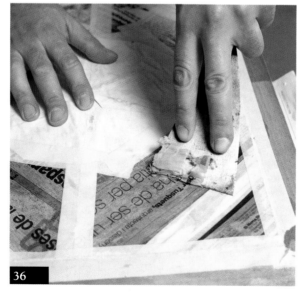

38. Once the veneer is dry, it is scraped to level it and clean any traces of glue. This is always done following the direction of the grain of the wood.

39. A varnish is used for the finish. It is applied in thin coats with a wide brush.

40. When the varnish is completely dry, it is sanded with fine sandpaper. In this case, an orbital sander is used.

41. After sanding, the entire surface is buffed with steel wool following the grain of the wood.

42. Wax is applied to the veneer with a cotton cloth.

43. The marquetry is buffed with a clean cotton cloth to polish it.

44. The completed piece. Notice the gloss resulting from the finishing process.

MIRROR FRAME

O n many occasions, doing marquetry work requires the application of decorative strips and bands. In this exercise, you will see how to apply the strips of wood veneer. These pieces can be found in specialized stores, and are available in different kinds of wood. The strips in this step-by-step project are simple narrow bands of wood, but you should be aware that decorative strips are also available, with Greek motifs for example. As a general rule, professionals use guillotines for cutting strips in their own shops.

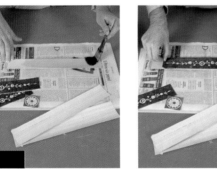

1. The project begins by laying out the actual dimensions of the mirror frame on a piece of paper and drawing the four side panels and the borders. A pencil and a long ruler are used for this.

2. Marquetry designs are selected and added to the drawing, making sure that they are centered in the previously drawn rectangles. These designs are simple drawings on paper.

3. Next, sheets of sycamore veneer with a uniform light color are covered with rabbit skin glue, using a wide brush, with a paper underneath to protect the work surface.

4. Then the paper sketches are placed on the veneer.

5. These are all pressed for a few minutes to achieve a good bond. As usual, the sheets are placed between two pieces of paper and two boards so that the veneer will not be damaged.

6. A small manual press can be used for pressing these pieces.

7. Meanwhile, we cut the dark background sheets for the marquetry from etimoe wood, using a metal straight edge and a cutting blade.

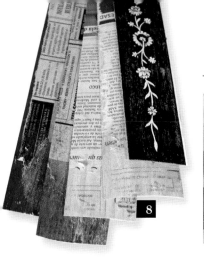

8. All the sheets are stacked, making sure that the one with the drawing is on top.

9. Next, the stack is nailed together. This is done on a board to prevent damage to the top table.

10. Then, the points of the nails that come through are cut off with pincers.

11. The nails are bent over for more holding power. This is done by placing the stack of veneer on a flat steel plate and striking the nails with a hammer.

12. A hole is made with a hand-held drill for a saw blade to pass through.

13. Once the blade is connected to the saw we begin cutting the stack of veneer. The stack is taken apart after sawing.

14. Next, we proceed with the shading of the different pieces, following the design drawing. We use tweezers to avoid burning our fingers.

15. After the shading is completed, the pieces are inserted in the background sheets using an awl.

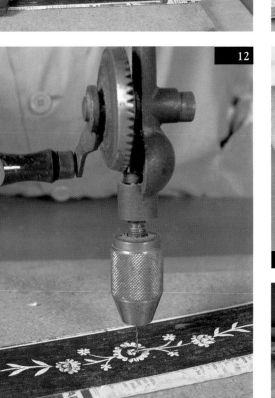

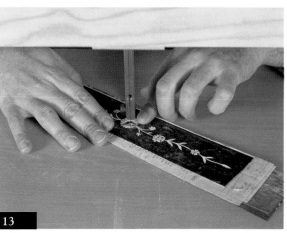

16. Paper brushed with rabbit skin glue is used to bond all of the pieces.

17. The pieces of paper are placed on the marquetry to secure all the parts.

18. The marquetry is turned over and the pieces are adjusted using the awl.

19. Then, the veneer for the corners is cut using a utility knife and a metal straight edge.

20. The dark background veneer pieces are made into stacks.

21. The stack is sawed and the pieces are carefully laid out on a tray.

22. The light colored pieces are inserted into the dark background pieces with an awl.

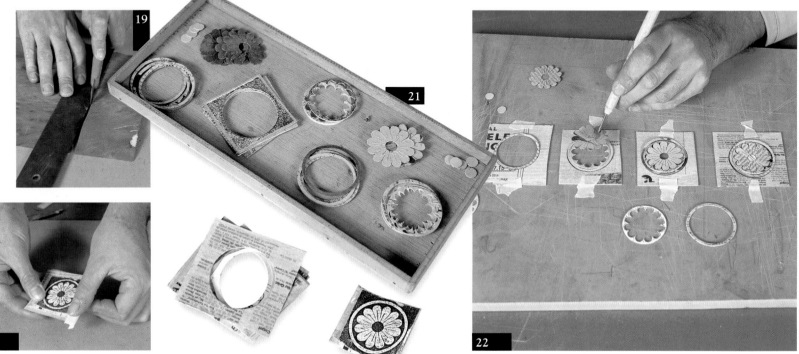

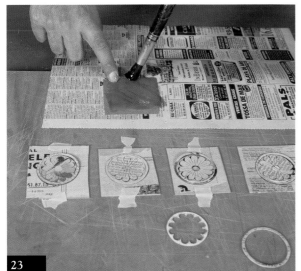

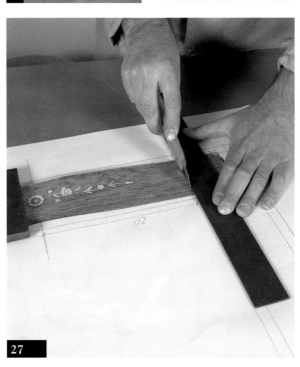

23. Pieces of paper are then brushed with rabbit skin glue.

24. The papers are placed on the different pieces, completely covering them. Light pressure should be applied with the fingers.

25. Adjust the pieces with the help of an awl so that they fit perfectly in the background veneer. Then, place them in the press.

26. Once the pieces are assembled and pressed, measurements are checked using the design drawing.

27. The sides and corners are cut using a metal straight edge and a knife, and the excess is removed.

28. Notice that all the pieces are cut out and put in their corresponding places according to the drawing.

29. A strip of masking tape is placed under the marquetry to hold the strips.

30. Then, the strips, which are of a lighter colored wood, are put in place.

31. A wider band of wood is placed next to the strip, and then pressed with a hammer in the direction of the grain.

32. The same process is repeated with all the pieces of marquetry. A 45 degree cut is made at the corners with a chisel.

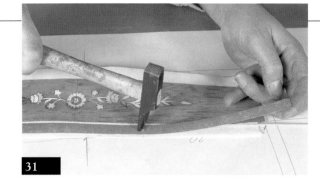

33. Afterwards, the strips are placed in the squares at the corners, and are held by the masking tape.

34. Then, the corner marquetry assemblies are put in place, and carefully pressed with the hammer.

35. To mount the marquetry to the backing board, both surfaces should be brushed with white glue.

36. A very strong bond is achieved by placing both in a press for at least ten hours.

37. When the glue is dry, the paper is removed by wetting it with a sponge soaked in water.

38. All the paper is removed using a scraper, being careful not to damage the marquetry.

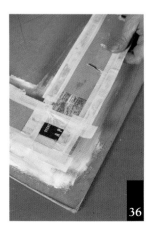

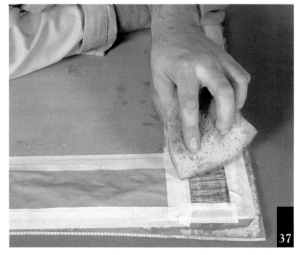

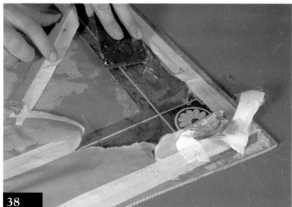

39. Once the paper is removed and the frame is dry, the veneer is smoothed and remnants of glue are removed with a scraper.

40. The inside of the frame is cut out with a saw, making straight cuts.

41. After gluing together a pine frame to accommodate the thickness of the mirror, the edges are sanded with a medium grade sandpaper.

42. The edges are finished by brushing them and some bands of veneer of the same width with contact cement.

43. The edge bands will bond after five minutes.

44. The different pieces of veneer are smoothed and any glue is removed using a scraper.

45. The finishing step consists of sanding and varnishing the entire frame.

46. The finished mirror frame.

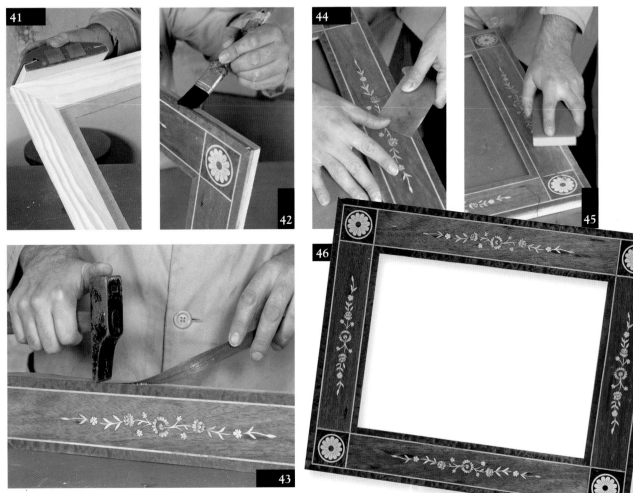

JEWELRY BOX

*S*ometimes *furniture or objects are made that are later decorated with some kind of ornamentation. In the following project, we have a plain wood box that is going to be used as a jewelry box. Yet, once it is covered with marquetry,* *it will have a greater value because of the decoration. In this step-by-step activity, we can appreciate the technique and difficulty involved in special woodwork.*

1. The box made by a woodworker has two parts: the box itself with its curved sides, and the lid.

2. Four turned wood feet will go on the bottom of the jewelry box. From this point on, the marquetry work begins.

3. We prepare the pieces of veneer that will serve as the base of the marquetry. Since they are only about 1/64 inch thick (0.5 mm), they need reinforcement. First, they are brushed with rabbit skin glue.

4. Then, newsprint is placed over the glued face.

5. Next, they are pressed between two boards held with clamps or with a book binding press. This step will give the veneer some flexibility.

6. While the different sheets of veneer are being pressed, we choose the design to be reproduced in marquetry, and we glue it to a piece of veneer.

7. The sheets of veneer should be stacked in the following order: the sheet with the design, the sheet of light colored sycamore for the light pieces and the dark background sheet of sapele pommele. This method is known as positive and negative.

8. The stack should be held in place with small nails so that it will not shift. It is important to note that the nails are always inserted in the face that has the newsprint.

9. After making a small hole with a drill in a line of the design, the saw blade is passed through and we begin cutting out the pieces.

10. The craftsman guides the stack with his hands while the saw continues its up and down movement. It is important to maintain the proper blade tension during the sawing process.

11. The pieces must be removed with the greatest of care.

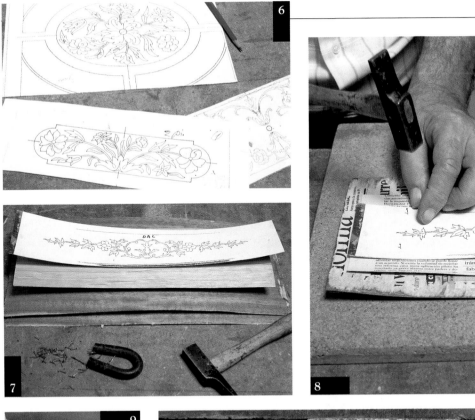

12. The white pieces are set aside while the dark pieces cut from the background are discarded.

13. All the pieces are arranged on a tray so that they will not be misplaced.

14. Then, we go on to shade the pieces by burying the part we wish to color in silica sand, which is in a fireproof container on top of a hotplate.

15. Long tweezers are used to remove the pieces from the sand without burning our hands.

16. A screwdriver is used to straighten the bent over nails so that the veneer stack can be taken apart.

17. The nails are then cut off using small pincers.

18. The heads of the nails are also cut off from the other side.

19. After cutting the nails, the sheets are separated.

20. Once they are apart we can see that the white pieces match the dark sheets.

21. The shaded pieces may now be inserted into the dark background sheet. An awl is used for this. Once they are all in place, a sheet of newsprint is glued over it with rabbit skin glue to keep the pieces from coming out.

22. Then, glue is applied to a sheet of reinforcing veneer.

23. The marquetry is bonded to it.

24. Notice that the newsprint acts as a reinforcement for the marquetry.

25. Newsprint is used so that the glue will not get on the press.

26. The packet is placed in the press under pressure.

27. When the glue is dry, after about 24 hours, the paper is loosened by wetting it with water.

28. The paper is then removed with a paint scraper.

29. Contact cement is applied to the lid and to the underside of the marquetry.

30. The marquetry is carefully pressed to the lid with a simple wood tool.

31. A scraper is again used to carefully remove any remnants of paper.

32. The edges and the surface of the marquetry are polished with sandpaper.

33. Next, the edges of the jewelry box are covered.

34. Contact cement is applied to the curved sides of the jewelry box the same way it was applied to the lid.

35. The marquetry is centered by hand and the overhanging veneer is cut off.

36. The next step is to attach the hinges. To do so, the positions of the holes are marked with an awl.

37. After sanding and varnishing all the parts, the jewelry box is finished.

TABLE TOP

The objective of this exercise is to demonstrate how to make an inlaid round table top. The procedures and required techniques are complex and demand a certain level of experience. In this step-by-step exercise, a mechanical screw press is used, as is commonly done in a marquetry workshop.

1. To begin the design, we draw two concentric circles: the one on the outside having a diameter equal to that of the table to be covered with the marquetry. Then, two perpendicular lines are drawn with a ruler dividing the circles into four equal parts.

2. Next, the outside ring between the two circles is divided into 32 equal segments, and the direction of the wood grain is marked on all of them. Colored pencils can be used for this step.

3. The background sheets are cut with a utility knife and a metal straight edge, following the triangular shapes of the four sections. In this case, elm burl is used.

4. In the same manner, sycamore veneer is cut to fit the quarters of the inner circle. The designs of the inner circle will be traced on them.

5. As you can see, the sycamore veneer is distinctively lighter than the elm burl.

6. One piece of sycamore is placed on the drawing, and the outline of the design is drawn on tracing paper. When one quarter is finished, it can be copied on white paper to make it easier to work with.

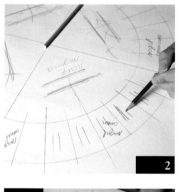

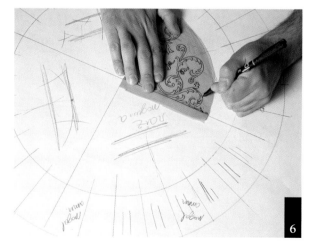

7. The copies are brushed with white glue and bonded to each of the master sheets. The master sheets add thickness to the stack of veneer.

8. Then, all the pieces are placed between two boards and inserted into a press for ten minutes.

9. After the pressing, the sheets are removed from the press and are tightly joined together with nails to make sure they stay in place.

10. The heads of the nails are cut off using pincers.

11. The nails are bent over, using a steel plate underneath the stack of veneer.

12. The pieces are then cut out. A hole is first made with a hand drill and a small bit on a line of the drawing.

13. Next, the saw blade is inserted through the hole and attached to the saw.

14. Much patience and concentration is required while cutting out the pieces. Keep in mind that the saw blade moves up and down, and that it is the marquetry that must be moved to guide the cut.

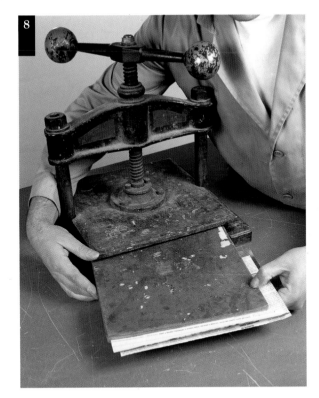

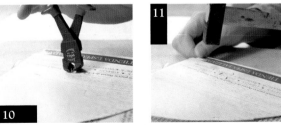

15. After sawing, the pieces are removed.

16. The stacks containing all the sheets of veneer are taken apart. This is done by using a screwdriver as a lever and being careful not to damage the wood.

17. After taking apart the packets, the dark veneer, which will decorate the background, is placed on a board and attached with nails.

18. The light colored pieces are inserted into the dark background using an awl.

19. After finishing the assembly, a few sheets of paper are brushed with rabbit skin glue.

20. The papers are placed on each of the marquetry pieces and pressed with the fingertips so that the nails come through the paper.

21. Then, the nails that hold the background to the wood board are removed and the marquetry is put into the press.

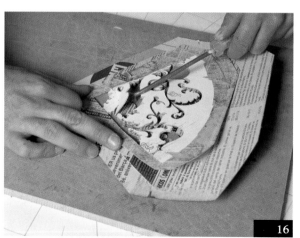

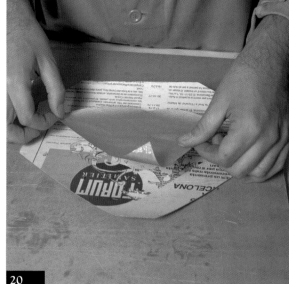

22. After about ten minutes in the press, the marquetry is removed and the perpendicular edges of the four pieces are cut.

23. Then, the pieces are joined together. A strip of masking tape is placed with the adhesive facing up and the sides to be joined are placed on it.

24. The pieces must meet perfectly; otherwise the quality of the project will be affected.

25. The seams of all the pieces are lightly pressed with a hammer.

26. The outside ring is then assembled. For this, 32 sections are cut and attached with masking tape on top of the previously drawn design.

27. The inside diameter of the ring is very carefully marked with a compass so as not to damage the veneer.

28. The inside of the ring is cut with a utility knife. This is done freehand, with as much accuracy as possible.

29. It is important to make sure that the seams in the ring match those of the background of the marquetry. A metal ruler is used for checking and centering the entire design.

30. Next, the circular band is attached to the background with nails.

31. Then, the width of the circular strip is marked with the compass, which should be perfectly centered.

32. The overhanging veneer is cut freehand using a knife.

33. The strip (previously cut with a guillotine cutter or utility knife) is inserted into the groove using a hammer. Notice that one end of the strip is held in place with masking tape.

34. Inserting the strip into the groove must be done slowly and carefully since the veneer can be easily damaged.

35. The marquetry and its backing are brushed with white glue.

36. After covering it with newspaper to prevent deterioration of the press, the entire marquetry is placed in the veneer press.

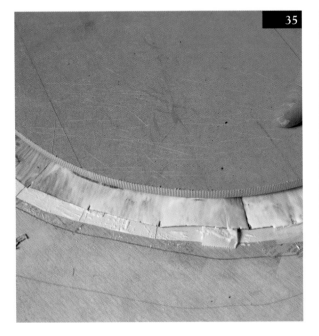

37. In this exercise, we are using a mechanical press that is controlled manually by tightening a screw.

38. After about four hours, the marquetry can be removed from the press.

39. In order to remove the paper bonded to the marquetry, it must first be dampened using a sponge soaked with water.

40. A spatula is then used to remove the paper, being careful not to damage the marquetry.

41. Once the marquetry dries, remnants of the paper and glue are removed with a scraper. The scraping process will also help level the thickness of the different pieces of veneer used to assemble the marquetry work.

42. After the top is attached to the base and the whole piece is varnished, the work is complete.

LANDSCAPE

*I*n this project, the typical processes of marquetry were rendered considerably easier by substituting other techniques. One example is the use of clamps for pressing the veneer. Nevertheless, it is important to keep in mind that the complexity of this step-by-step activity lies in its composition, given the great variety of the pieces, which turns the assembly into a jigsaw puzzle.

However, the magnificent results will compensate for the great effort required.

The veneers used in creating this work are: sycamore for the background; elm burl for the tree and for the rocks; oak, cebrano, and sycamore for the mountain; erable dyed green for the foliage; coral for the hat on the male figure; and ebony for the cape of the male figure.

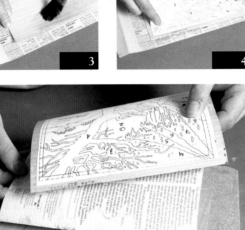

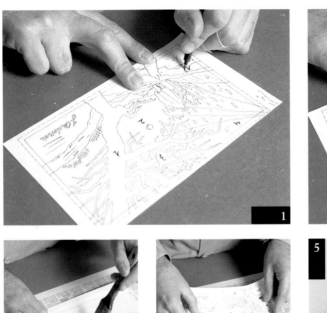

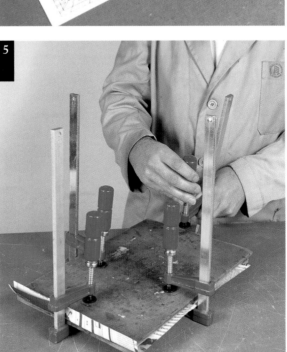

1. One of the tasks that must be carried out before the actual creation of the marquetry is choosing the design and making the drawing to be used. The drawing is made on paper and the pieces are numbered. Then a copy is made.

2. Next, the different pieces to be cut for the marquetry are colored using shades similar to those of the veneers that will be used.

3. Then, the master sheet is coated with rabbit skin glue already heated in a double boiler. A wide brush is used to spread the glue over the entire surface of the veneer.

4. Next, the drawing is placed over the surface of the master sheet of veneer and lightly pressing it by hand.

5. The marquetry is then placed between two boards and pressure is applied with the help of four clamps.

6. Then, the stack of veneer is assembled in the following order: first, the master sheet with the drawing; second, the veneer for framing the pieces, and finally, the reinforcing sheet of veneer.

7. Some small nails are tapped into place with a hammer to hold the veneer stack together.

8. Before cutting out the veneer, a small hole is made with a hand drill where the saw blade will be inserted.

9. Next, all the pieces are cut out. As the pieces are cut, they should be arranged on a tray.

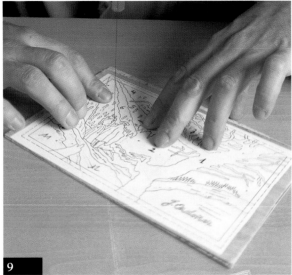

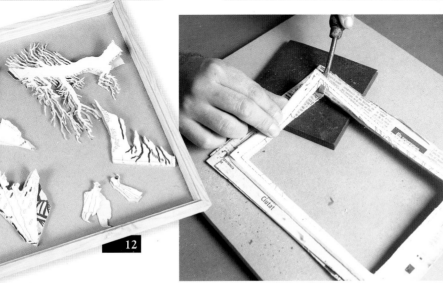

10. In this type of marquetry where many cuts are required, the outside of the different areas are cut out first, then the inside cutting is done.

11. Notice how all the pieces are laid out in perfect order on a tray, with enough distance between them so that they will not get mixed up.

12. All the pieces that make up the design are now completely cut and laid out on the tray.

13. The rest of the stack is dis-assembled using a screwdriver.

14. If any piece is broken during the cutting or assembling process, it will not be noticed after the marquetry is glued together.

15. A piece of veneer is brushed with glue, taking care to spread it evenly over the entire surface. All the pieces of the same color will be bonded to this piece of veneer.

16. The pieces of the same color are placed on the sheet of veneer with an awl. It is very important to pay attention to the direction of the grain.

17. The pieces are pressed by placing them between two boards and holding them together with two clamps.

18. A piece of the veneer in the color chosen for the pieces is then cut with a utility knife and a metal straight edge.

19. A stack is then made using a backing veneer, the colored veneer cut in the previous step, and over that the veneer being used for the pattern.

20. Masking tape is attached all around the perimeter of the stack to keep the pieces from coming apart.

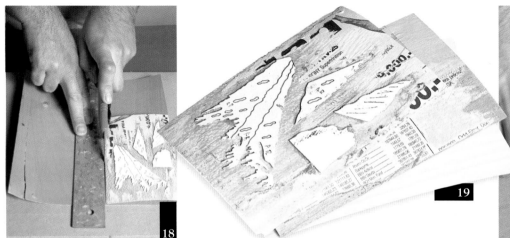

21. Then necessary holes are made with a hand drill for the saw blade to pass through.

22. Next, the inside shapes of the pieces are cut out. Keep in mind that the smaller the pieces are, the greater the risk of losing them.

23. Notice the position of the hands while cutting out the small inside pieces.

24. The outside of the pieces are cut, using as much accuracy as possible when cutting out the profiles.

25. Once the figures seen in the photograph are cut out, the rest of the pieces are cut in the same way.

26. The pieces held with tweezers are inserted into the heated silica sand to create shading.

27. The longer the veneer is left in the silica sand, the darker the shadow tone will be.

28. The pieces are removed from the sand with tweezers.

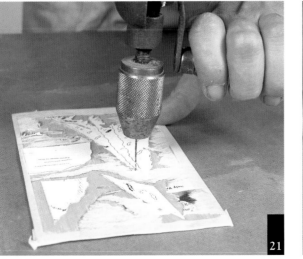

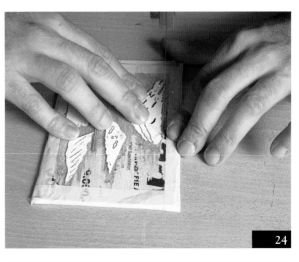

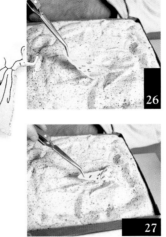

29. The veneer is checked against the colored drawing to see if the shading is correct.

30. Then, the piece of veneer that acts as a frame is attached to a board with masking tape. The drawing with the numbers should be kept nearby.

31. The pieces are then inserted into their places with the help of an awl.

32. Next, the paper is brushed with rabbit skin glue heated in a double boiler, making sure the entire surface is covered.

33. The paper is placed over the assembled marquetry and pressed with the hands so that it adheres properly. This step ensures that the pieces will stay in place.

34. Then, the board is turned over and, with the help of an awl, the positioning of the pieces is adjusted.

35. A backing board is then brushed with white glue.

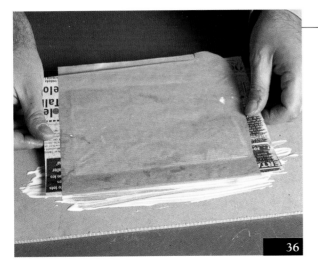

36. The assembled marquetry is bonded to the backing board.

37. To guarantee a good bond between the marquetry and the backing board, both are placed into a press and left for a minimum of two hours.

38. Notice how the paper that covers the marquetry is dampened with a sponge soaked in water.

39. Then, using a paint scraper, all the paper is removed, leaving the marquetry visible.

40. Once the marquetry is dry, it is scraped to level the pieces of veneer and remove traces of glue and paper.

41. The final step is to cut around the perimeter of the backing board using a skill saw, discarding the remaining pieces.

42. Varnishing and framing the marquetry gives the composition a beautiful finished look.

BOOKSTAND

*I*n the following exercise, we demonstrate step-by-step the design and development process of a work of marquetry created for a wood bookstand. At the end of this exercise, we show a variation of this marquetry project as applied to a mirror frame.

The veneers used to create this marquetry are: bubinga wood, with a reddish tone, erable and sycamore, which have been dyed in salmon and green tones.

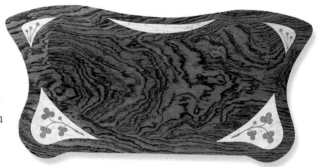

1. The exercise begins by creating the design to be used. A full-size drawing of the design is made. Notice how a template is used as an aid in drawing the required curves on the paper.

2. Then, the design motifs are drawn inside the outlines in the proportion suited to the amount of space available.

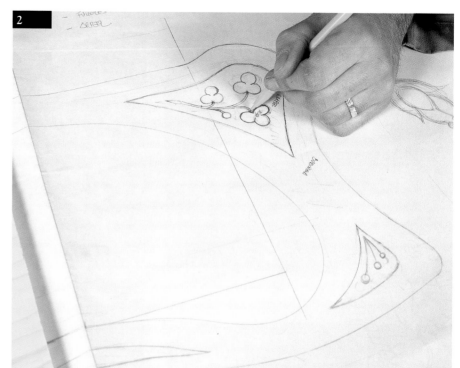

3. A master sheet of veneer is then selected and brushed with rabbit skin glue.

4. The drawings are glued to the master. In order to guarantee a good bond, press the veneer and paper for about ten minutes.

5. Then, choose the type and color of the veneers that will make up the marquetry work.

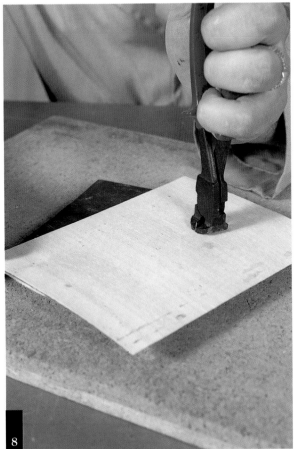

8. After that, the points of the nails are cut off and tapped with a hammer to rivet them. It is a good idea to put a piece of steel plate underneath the stack before the nails are cut and riveted.

9. Then, a hole is made in the inside of the design with a hand drill and a piercing saw blade is threaded through it. In this way, the process of cutting out the different pieces can begin.

10. As the pieces are cut out, they are removed using an awl and then placed in order on a tray.

11. Once the inside pieces are cut out, the outside of the design is sawn. The process is the same as for the inside pieces.

12. The pieces are laid out on a sheet of wood that will act as the backing board for the bookstand. Then, the outline is marked with a pencil.

6. Next, the sawing stack is assembled. The sheet with the design is placed on top of all the veneer sheets. Special care must be taken to place the sheets of veneer in the direction of the grain as indicated in the design drawing.

7. Then, the stack of veneer is nailed together. It is placed on a cork base and a number of nails are driven in to hold it tightly.

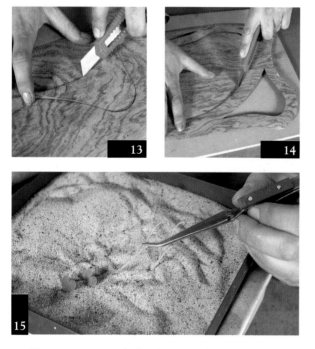

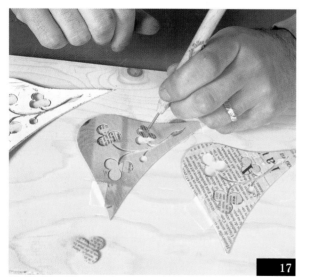

13. The veneer is cut out freehand using a utility knife. This task is especially complex, given that some of the cutting will go across the grain, which could cause the veneer to split if great care is not taken.

14. The center of the bookstand is cut out in the shape of a kidney. The utility knife is again used for this task.

15. Then, the pieces to be shaded are selected and placed into a tray of hot silica sand. Exercise caution and use the tweezers to avoid burning your fingers.

16. Remember that the veneer pieces, both sawn and shaded, should be kept organized on a tray.

17. During assembly of the marquetry, the pieces are picked up one at a time with an awl and inserted in their corresponding places within the body of the marquetry work.

18. Once the assembly is finished, a piece of paper is brushed with rabbit skin glue, being careful not to damage the top of the work table.

23. A piece of paper the same size as the marquetry is then brushed with rabbit skin glue.

24. The piece of paper is placed over the marquetry work and smoothed and pressed by hand to bond all areas.

25. The marquetry work is turned over and the pieces are adjusted by applying light pressure with the fingertips on the different parts of the frame.

19. Next, the paper is placed over the marquetry and pressed lightly with the fingertips in order to secure the loose pieces.

20. Then, the marquetry work is turned over and the pieces are adjusted using an awl.

21. Following this, the sheets of veneer are placed between two boards and are then put into a manual press and left for about ten minutes.

22. After the pressing, the work is laid on a board and all the different pieces are assembled with the help of a hammer and a few nails.

26. Next, white glue is applied to a board, and spread evenly over the entire surface with a brush.

27. The marquetry, which has also been brushed with glue, is then placed on top of the backing board and put into a press for approximately four hours. It is important that the press exert a uniform pressure over the entire surface.

28. Once the glue is dry, the marquetry is taken from the press and is dampened using a sponge soaked with water. This will help make the removal of the newsprint easier.

29. A paint scraper is used carefully to peel off the paper.

30. When the veneer is dry, the scraping can be done, moving in the same direction as the wood grain.

31. The outline of the bookstand is cut with the saw. This task must be carried out very carefully so the marquetry will not be damaged.

32. The bookstand after varnishing.

33. A support constructed on the back side of the bookstand.

34. In order to use the same marquetry piece as a mirror frame, the back side should be veneered, and an inset then cut into the back of the board, just as the photograph illustrates.

35. A mirror cut to fit the frame is then set into place.

36. Then, a cover, also cut to fit into the frame, is installed over the mirror.

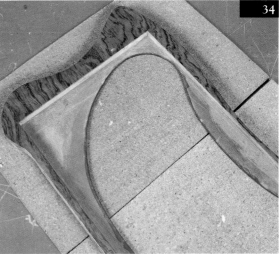

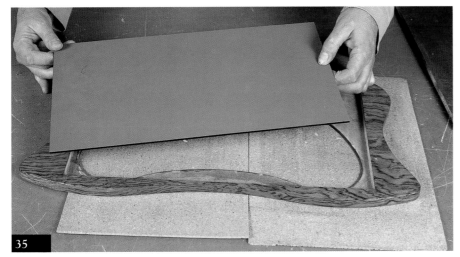

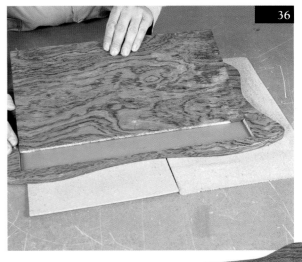

37. Brass hardware is installed to hold the cover in place. One piece of hardware, which can be seen in the photograph, offers a loop for hanging the mirror.

38. A view of the completed mirror. Proof of the versatility of marquetry, which can be applied to any type of furniture piece or wooden object.

GLOSSARY

Awl. A steel tool with a point at one end. It is used for making holes and marking pieces.

Brush. A flat, wide brush or a fine artist's paint brush used to spread stain or varnish on wood.

Buffing pad. Cheesecloth or fibers wrapped in a cloth used to apply shellac or varnish to wood in very fine coats.

Chisel. A steel tool used by a woodworker to carve wood.

Clamp. A steel tool used to apply pressure to a piece on a workbench or to hold two pieces together.

Contact cement. A type of adhesive used for repair work in cases where it is difficult to use clamps to hold pieces in place. It is also commonly used to bond sheets of melamine and for veneering wood.

Fibers. The tubes that grow vertically in the trunk of a tree through which the sap flows.

Finish. The last treatment applied to a wood object or piece of furniture.

Grain. The fiber of a piece of wood.

Inlay. A technique that consists of inserting pieces of wood, bone, metal, or other materials into wood for decorative purposes.

Knot. A manifestation in the wood resulting from the point of intersection between the branch and the trunk of a tree.

Marquetry. A technique for creating decorative surfaces by gluing pieces of veneer made of different woods or other materials to a wood backing or piece of furniture.

Rabbit skin glue. An adhesive of animal origin, made from the hide and bones of the animal. In the past it was often used for bonding pieces of wood. Nowadays, it is not used very much, except for veneering wood. It is available in the form of flakes or fine granules, which must be dissolved in hot water in a double boiler.

Sanding. The action of rubbing a surface with sandpaper to make it smooth.

Scraper. A steel tool, with sharpened edges, used for scraping and smoothing wood surfaces.

Scraping. A method used to strip or polish wood before it is varnished or waxed.

Sketch. A drawing made freehand.

Varnish. A solution of gum or resin in a solvent that, when applied on a surface, dries and forms a coating that is more or less glossy, transparent, and waterproof.

Veneer. A very fine sheet of wood, usually between 1/128 and 1/8 inch (0.2 and 3 mm) applied over other woods as a covering layer.

Veneered. A piece of wood that is covered with veneer.

Wax. An animal or vegetable substance that is used as a finishing coat on wood surfaces.

White glue (also known as "Carpenter's Glue"). A polyvinyl acetate adhesive. It is one of the easiest adhesives to use, works very well for all uses, and is not toxic.